MY
HOPE
JOURNAL

MY
HOPE
JOURNAL

Companion to
THE SONG OF MY HOPE
for Connection Groups

BETSY KAY RIDGWAY

1603 Capitol Ave., Suite 310 Cheyenne, Wyoming USA 82001
1-888-980-6523 | admin@urlinkpublishing.com

URLink Print and Media is committed to excellence in the publishing industry.

Book design copyright © 2023 by URLink Print and Media. All rights reserved.

Published in the United States of America

Library of Congress Control Number: 2023920723
ISBN 978-1-68486-581-9 (Paperback)
ISBN 978-1-68486-582-6 (Digital)

23.10.23

Welcome!

I created this journal as a companion to my book, The Song of My Hope. *You will love the way this guide spurs you on to deeper conversations about your life and your faith. You can also benefit by using this as your daily devotional.*

My desire is to see you connect more deeply with God and friends. Our Lord is the Creator of Hope! No matter what you may be struggling with, give yourself permission to draw closer with friends and be willing to dip your feet into the Living Water.

This is one secret to feeling refreshed and full of hope! If you invest a little time each day filling up with God's Word and sharing with an open heart, you will reap the benefits of a closer walk with Jesus and deeper friendships!

May God inspire you with hope, as your joy overflows into singing a new song!

*"May the God of Hope fill you with
all joy and peace as you trust in Him,
so that you may overflow with Hope
by the power of the Holy Spirit."*

Romans 15:13

INTRODUCTION

*"He put a new song in my mouth,
a song of praise to our God; many
will see, have awe and will trust
in the LORD." Psalm 40:3*

What "new song" do you want to sing? Has the Lord called you to a vocation or a mission?

What are your passions/talents?

How can you weave your passions and talents into your hopes, dreams and desires to fulfill your calling?

DAY 1
DEEP FEAR

"Be strong, and let your heart take courage all you who hope in the Lord." (Psalm 31:24)

Recall a time of deep fear. How did you respond to that fear?

How could you have responded differently?

What plan could you implement to fight fear you might experience in the future?

DAY 2
REGRET/SHAME

"My soul finds rest in God; my hope comes from Him." (Psalm 62:5)

Describe a time you regretted a past experience.

Recall a time you felt shame.

Satan is the condemner and his mission is to imprison you with shame. Give this burden up to the Lord now. Find a Scripture that will help you know the freedom Christ came to give you.

DAY 3
DEEP DISAPPOINTMENT

"When anxiety was great within me, Your comfort brought me joy." (Psalm 94:19)

Many of us suffer from anxiety on one level or another. How's yours on a scale of one to ten?

We deal with anxiety in a variety of ways. Unhealthy ways could be oversleeping, overeating and more. Can you name anymore?

Like taking a walk with a friend, what are some other healthy ways we can deal with anxiety?

DAY 4
TRUSTING GOD

"Now faith is being sure of what we hope for, and certain of what we do not see." (Hebrews 11:1)

Was there a time in your life you were believing for a good outcome? If you did not receive the good outcome, how did you cope?

Where do we sometimes put our faith? What gets in our way?

Can you share about an experience that strengthened your faith?

DAY 5
LACK OF FAITH

*"Whoever dwells in the shelter of the
Most High will rest in the shadow of
the Almighty. I will say of the LORD,
'He is my refuge and my fortress, my
God, in Whom I trust.'" (Psalm 91:1-2)*

Can you describe a time you experienced a
lack of faith?

Did you feel guilty for your lack of faith?

What did you do that helped strengthen your
faith?

DAY 6
CURIOUS COURAGE

"Be strong and courageous. Do not be afraid or terrified because of them, for the LORD your God goes with you; He will never leave you nor forsake you." (Deuteronomy 31:6-8)

How would you define courage?

Describe a time someone you know acted courageously. Feel free to share about yourself.

How can we build up our "courage muscles"?

DAY 7
HOPELESSNESS

"For You make me glad by Your deeds, LORD, I sing for joy at what Your hands have done." (Psalm 92:4)

From The Song of My Hope, read "Supplement A" out loud. Which sentence(s) holds true for you?

Read Psalm 147:11, Proverbs 13:12 and Romans 15:13. Do you have a favorite scripture on hope?

Describe a time when you experienced hopelessness. What helped or didn't help you?

DAY 8
FEELING LOST

"For I know the plans I have for you," declares the LORD, "plans to prosper you and not to harm you, plans to give you a hope and a future." (Jeremiah 29:11)

Describe a time in your life when you felt like you were drifting through life without a purpose.

Has God given you a task, a mission, a job? What is it? How did you react when you were given a job, task or mission?

I waited seven years after God asked me to write *The Song of My Hope*. Have you delayed doing a job God has asked you to do? How can others support you so you can accomplish it?

DAY 9
STRESSED

Define stress. Where does stress materialize in your body?

What is the opposite of stress?

Are there verses that are helpful for you when you feel stressed or worried?

DAY 10
OVERWHELMED

"But the fruit of the Spirit is love, joy, peace, forbearance, kindness, goodness, faithfulness, gentleness and self-control. Against such thing there is no law." (Galatians 5:22-23)

How do you react when you are overwhelmed? What happens over the long-term?

What are some things you do to feel more peaceful?

DAY 11
NOT IN CONTROL

"And I will give eternal life to them, and they will never perish; and no one will snatch them out of My hand." (John 10:28)

How do you react when something seems beyond your control?

What did you struggle with at that time?

Find a few comforting Scriptures that you can lean on during these times in the future.

DAY 12
CRITICISM

"You then, my child, be strengthened by the grace that is in Christ Jesus." (2 Timothy 2:1)

How is destructive criticism different from constructive criticism?

How do you react to criticism?

Proverbs 19:20 says, *"Listen to advice and accept correction, and in the end you will be wise."* Was there a time when you experienced helpful criticism that was a blessing?

DAY 13
LACK OF JOY

*"Your love has given me great joy
and encouragement, because you
have refreshed the hearts of the
Lord's people." (Philemon 1:7)*

Describe the last time you experienced a lack of joy.

What do you think are some causes of a lack of joy?

What can we do to experience more joy?

DAY 14
WEAKNESS

*"God is our refuge and strength,
and ever-present help in
trouble." (Psalm 46:1)*

How do you suppose our strength comes from using God as our refuge?

What does it mean to "rest in the Lord"? What are the benefits to this type of rest?

How is our faith connected to resting in the Lord? Describe a time you were able to "rest in the Lord" and let God be in control.

DAY 15
EMBARRASSMENT

"Let the Light of the Lord shine upon me. The LORD fills my heart with joy! I sleep in peace because the LORD makes me dwell in safety." (Psalm 4:6-8)

The root of embarrassment is pride. We want to be seen in a positive light by others. Describe a time when you experienced embarrassment.

How did you handle that embarrassment?

Letting go of pride and allowing ourselves to be transparent can sometimes be uncomfortable. Let the light of the Lord shine in you and fill you with inner beauty! You will feel more peaceful!

DAY 16
INSECURITY

*"And my God will supply all your
needs according to His riches in glory
in Christ Jesus." (Philippians 4:19)*

How is lack of faith a factor in our insecurity?

What kinds of things do you rely on for
security? How is that working for you?

God promises to meet all of our needs, filled
up and overflowing! How can we change
from feeling insecure to feeling confident in
God's supply?

DAY 17
FRUSTRATION

"My son/daughter, keep your father's command and do not forsake your mother's teaching." (Proverbs 6:20)

Frustration can occur when your needs/desires are not being met. What is a common response to frustration?

Since frustration is a response, how can we tame this emotional response?

Having a plan so you can "act" instead of "react" is crucial to keeping your cool. If you have a plan, please share it now.

DAY 18
WORRY

"Peace is what I leave with you; it is My own peace that I give you. I do not give it as the world does. Do not be worried and upset; do not be afraid." (John 14:27)

What are some of the causes of worry?

What is the spiritual root of fear?

What does Jesus have to say about lack of faith?

DAY 19
DISTRESS

*"I have said these things to you, that
in Me you may have peace. In the
world you will have tribulation.
But take heart; I have overcome
the world." (John 16:33)*

Compare definitions of "stress" and "distress".
Discuss ways they are different.

Distress is a body's failed attempt to deal with
stress. An example of distress is depression.
How does distress affect you?

In the scripture above, what are some ways
Jesus directs our path to peace?

DAY 20
HUMILIATION

"Humble yourselves, therefore, under God's mighty hand, that He may lift you up in due time." (1 Peter 5:6)

Describe a time you experienced humiliation.

What was your reaction to this humiliation? Do you still recount this memory vividly?

What does Peter say about the remedy for humiliation? What does it mean to humble yourself?

DAY 21
LACKING WISDOM

"Do not forsake wisdom, and she will protect you; love her, and she will watch over you." (Proverbs 4:6)

What is the underlying difference between worldly wisdom and Godly wisdom?

How often do you seek the Lord's wisdom when you have a problem?

How can Godly wisdom protect us and watch over us?

DAY 22
TERROR

*"The LORD makes firm the steps
of the one who delights in Him;
though he may stumble, he will not
fall, for the LORD upholds him
with His hand." (Psalm 37:23-24)*

Our body's natural reaction to terror is fight, flight or freezing. How can we train this natural reaction so that we may think more clearly in an emergency?

Read 2ⁿᵈ Timothy 1:7 *"For God has not given us the spirit of fear; but of <u>power</u>, and of <u>love</u>, and a <u>sound mind</u>."* Philippians 4:7 *"And the <u>peace of God</u>, which transcends all understanding, <u>will guard your hearts and your minds</u> in Christ Jesus.*

Declare these two versus daily to train your mind to react peacefully during a time of terror and fear.

DAY 23
JOYFUL

*"But let all who take refuge
in You be glad; let them ever
sing for joy." (Psalm 5:11)*

What is God's "recipe" for joy?

What actions do you take to feel joyful?

How can we use our overflowing joy to cheer
others?

DAY 24
BROKENHEARTED

"The LORD is near to the brokenhearted and saves the crushed in spirit." (Psalm 34:18)

Please share about a time you experienced a broken heart.

What helped you through that difficult time?

How can we offer comfort to others going through a heartbreaking time?

LEGAL PROBLEMS

*"For there is one God, and one mediator
also between God and men, the man
Christ Jesus." (1 Timothy 2:5)*

Have you ever experienced a serious
disagreement? Share about it.

What does the Lord ask us to do for our
"enemies"?

What scriptures would you suggest to help
you in this situation?

DAY 26
FORGIVENESS

"The mouth speaks from the overflow of the heart." (Matthew 12:34)

Although the story from Chapter 26 was on the lighter side, we often hold onto deep hurts, sometimes for years. What can happen to our health as a result?

What does God's Word say about forgiveness?

Let's agree that since God created us, He knows how to keep us healthy and full of joy. Forgiveness is one of the secrets. Let's rely on His wisdom and make a decision to see the person as Jesus does, and forgive.

DAY 27
NEEDING COMFORT

"Be completely humble and gentle;
be patient, bearing with one
another in love." (Ephesians 4:2)

Share about a time when you needed comfort.

How did you find comfort?

It seems that people are very competent in many areas and this makes it difficult to ask for help. Let's make a commitment to this group that you will ask when you are in need of some comfort, prayer and fellowship.

DAY 28
GUIDANCE

"I will teach you the way you should go; I will instruct you and advise you." (Psalm 32:8)

Scriptures are full of wisdom in the area of guidance. Find one that speaks to you.

Was there a time when you needed guidance? Please share.

Before asking a friend, make sure you ask God first for guidance. Years ago, I heard this wise statement, "Go to the Throne before the phone!" What do you normally do when you need guidance?

DAY 29
DECISIONS

"Your Word is a lamp to guide me and a light for my path." (Psalm 119:105)

Now that we are forming a new habit and going to God first for wisdom on a decision, how can we know God has spoken to us?

Have you ever experienced God speaking to you through scriptures, through a friend, or even something on TV? God can talk to us through many means! Name some of the ways He talks to you.

Have you heard God clearly speak to you regarding a decision you put before Him in prayer?

DAY 30
PROTECTION

"For He will command His angels concerning you, to guard you in all your ways." (Psalm 91:11)

Chapter 7 "Hovering Angels" talks about our experience with angels. Have you had an encounter with angels or known someone who did?

Read Psalm 34:7, Psalm 91:1, and Psalm 103:20. According to these Scriptures, what is their job?

Let's put our faith and trust in God to protect us when we need it. This will bring us hope and joy for our present and for our future!

CLOSING DAY

*"Hope delayed makes the heart
sick, but a longing fulfilled is a
tree of life" (Proverbs 13:12)*

There are suggestions in "Supplement D" at
the end of *The Song of My Hope*. Briefly review
them.

Are there any that you would like to try? Share
which one.

What are some things you do to stay close to
God?

*My prayer is that you have
found a pathway to finding hope
and how to keep it alive!*

*God bless you as you continue to seek
hope and joy with a song in your heart!*